*How to Reduce Business Losses from
Employee Theft and Customer Fraud*

HOW TO REDUCE BUSINESS LOSSES FROM EMPLOYEE THEFT AND CUSTOMER FRAUD

ALFRED N. WEINER

ALMAR PRESS
4105 MARIETTA DRIVE
VESTAL, NEW YORK 13850

Library of Congress Cataloging-in-Publication Data

Weiner, Alfred N., 1924–
    How to reduce business losses from employee theft and
    customer fraud / Alfred N. Weiner

    p. cm.   ·

    Includes bibliographical references and index.
    ISBN 0-930256-23-9 (pbk. : alk. paper)
1. Employee theft – United States – Prevention.
2. Retail trade – Security measures – United States.
3. Business losses – United States – Prevention. I. Title.
HF5549.5.E43W45 1997
658.4'73 – DC21

First printing....March 1997

Printed in the United States of America

Book design by Gimore Design

This book is dedicated to my wife, Marilyn, who provided the encouragement and understanding to help me complete this book.

CONTENTS

Acknowledgements

My thank you to Dianna Weiner for her detailed analysis of the initial manuscript, Georganne Gillete for proofreading the final manuscript and Jean Levenson of Sentry Alarms for advice and information pertaining to business security systems.

1.0   INTRODUCTION

Purpose and Use of This Book.

Do you know where you have the greatest actual or potential loss in your business? Not all of the thieves are on the streets of the towns and cities in the U.S.A. Many more thieves spend their time in your office and plant. There, although considered to be honest citizens, these employees pilfer whatever is available. This dishonesty occurs in many forms and techniques in retail, wholesale, and manufacturing businesses.

For example, crime in retail business has grown to an estimated enormous $25 to $30 billion a year according to the U.S. Department of Commerce and other crime reporting sources. These data are based on merchandise inventories and other business audits. Exact data and information are difficult to obtain because employers do not always report their losses. They may be afraid of civil liability, damaging the company reputation, or legal restrictions. This fear of public exposure is especially true in the financial sector. When considering your customers, on an annual basis, more than 63 billion checks are written on an estimated 200 million checking accounts at 10,000 commercial banks,

10,000 credit unions, 2,000 savings and loans, and many other financial organizations. There are more than 1.6 billion retail transactions conducted with credit cards. As a result of all these transactions, the misuse of checks and credit cards is abundant and present a serious problem to any business.

Crime in the wholesale and manufacturing businesses has grown to an estimated $15 to $20 billion a year including the estimated $7 billion lost each year by motor carriers. One study projects the economic impact of crime on business, at its current rate of growth, will exceed $100 billion a year by the year 2000.

You must understand that the direct costs and effects of employee theft and customer fraud must be considered. The largest tangible factor is the cost of business insurance. The huge increases in premiums have been an important factor in the closing of many businesses in addition to the significant losses of money and merchandise. Another important aspect of the added expense to businesses is the cost of increased security in the form of security personnel and security equipment. All of these costs are passed on to the consumer in the form of higher prices for the merchandise that is sold.

Within a business there are indirect costs resulting from employee theft in the form of decreased productivity by employees, loss of morale, decreased product quality, and damage to the business image when the problem becomes public knowledge.

This book provides an easy-to-use review of the most important factors required to eliminate the largest source of these losses—theft by employees and the next-largest source of losses—customer fraud. For wholesalers, distributors, and manufacturers there is the added problem of burglary and robbery. This examination of the actual or potential losses in your business—regardless of the type of business—will help you to understand your management responsibility and the complexity of the problems involved.

One important factor that should be considered in helping to keep all of this information in proper perspective is the extent to which you, as the employer, considers any particular loss as theft. A deliberate increase in travel expenses on an expense account or the improper extension of overtime hours may not be considered as theft by every employer. There are other situations, such as extending break periods, improper absence, being late, or the incorrect use of sick leave that may not be considered as theft in the same classification as the removal of company property and products. Similarly, the use of company services such as unauthorized use of telephones, copy machines, computers, and other equipment may be considered as a more or less serious problem in various companies.

Your reaction to this information should be based on your company viewpoint as to the importance of the problems that are described.

To help you examine your knowledge of these crime problems and how they affect your business, we have provided three short easy-to-use checklists for you. These checklists will help you to begin a systematic approach to the application of the anticrime procedures that are given in this book.

A *CRIME DATA CHECKLIST* begins a self-analysis of management knowledge and actions pertaining to crime in your business.

A *CRIME AWARENESS CHECKLIST* examines the existing anticrime procedures in your business.

An *EMPLOYEE THEFT CHECKLIST AND GUIDE-LINES* is a detailed analysis of employee theft and procedures for its elimination in your business.

Also included is information for you to understand the use of bad checks, improper use of credit cards, and how to avoid these losses. In addition, there are other sources of immediate help, including trade and business associations, anticrime periodicals, a detailed list of state government planning agencies and U.S. government agencies.

NOTE TO THE READER

This book is intended to provide you with an overview of ideas on how to reduce your business losses. The text is not comprehensive on each topic. We suggest that you contact the sources indicated in the text for additional information. Also your bookstore and/or public library can provide more information based on the Bibliographic listing included in this book.

PURPOSE AND USE OF THIS BOOK

To combat employee theft the first consideration and responsibility of the individual business is to examine its own anticrime procedures. Each businessperson, whether representing one small business or a part of a large business organization, must plan and act to withstand the direct effects of this crime problem.

The information in this book will provide business management with an effective and systematic approach to the application of anticrime procedures. The majority of this information can be used for all retail, wholesale, and manufacturing businesses.

An essential feature for the success of this systematic approach is a positive commitment by **management to the reduction of losses which is in turn conveyed to and understood by the employees. In addition, within the retail businesses the employees must understand they have the responsibility to be certain that improper practices by customers are not tolerated.**

Beginning with this overall anticrime commitment, the next essential step is a self-analysis of management knowledge and actions.

Using the Checklists

While not requiring extensive time to complete, the information provided by the checklists will establish your overall awareness of the existing anticrime procedures that are being used in the business.

With this knowledge, a comparison can be made to the procedures described in this book. As a result, you will be able to carefully examine any of the actual or potential employee and customer crime techniques that are being used and their impact on the business. Then you can begin the additional procedures suggested in this book to eliminate losses.

While considering and implementing the use of additional anticrime procedures, you must also consider the attitude and relationship of the employee(s) to the **existing** anticrime procedures. You must also understand how the implementation of **new** procedures will influence their business operations and attitudes toward the business. Suggestions for the consideration of these employee responses are included within the description of the various procedures and the *EMPLOYEE THEFT CHECKLIST AND GUIDELINES* under the heading *IMPROVED COMMUNICATIONS* will help you.

First, there should be an analysis of the **internal** anticrime procedures for the business. Second, if you are responsible for a retail business then you should include an analysis of the business vulnerability to the major *external* sources of losses described as BAD CHECKS AND CREDIT CARD LOSSES.

Completing the analysis for the internal and external anticrime procedures on an individual business basis, You should look to the benefits that are available through combining of efforts with other businesses within your community and others within your same field of interest. For this effort, the other businesses in the same field of interest should not be considered as competitors. They are all businesses working together to a common goal. These anticrime procedures at the level of group action are under the headings of *WHAT THE COMMUNITY SHOULD DO* and Lists of Contacts in *BUSINESS ASSOCIATIONS THAT CAN HELP YOU.*

These sources include:
— Trade associations that will provide help and advice.
— Periodicals that offer the latest information for anticrime procedures.
— State and local government agencies that can be contacted for assistance.
— Department of Commerce investigation of crime in business and its recommendations.
— State planning agencies with specific offices to be contacted for assistance.

Begin the Checklists

Pages 9 through 18 include the **three checklists** with the questions, answers, and information required to begin an analysis of the existing anticrime procedures and the suggested application of required additional procedures.

2.0   CRIME DATA CHECKLIST

Underline the answer you believe correct.

1. Crime annually costs American businesses approximately (a) $30 million (b) $30 billion (c) $50 billion

2. The major area of loss for business is (a) Shoplifting (b) Burglary (c) Arson (d) Employee theft

3. The business sector that annually has the greatest loss is (a) Manufacturing (b) Retailing (c) Services (d) Wholesaling (e) Transportation

4. Business annually spends for preventive measures (a) $450 million (b) $950 million (c) $6 billion

5. Annual cost of crime per individual adult is (a) $20 (b) $100 (c) $300 (d) $600

6. Recent dollar crime loss calculated as a ratio of corporate profit was (a) 2% (b) 7% (c) 15% (d) 45%

7. Between 1986 and 1996 the number of burglaries increased (a) 12% (b) 65% (c) 125% (d) 182%

8. An acceptable level of inventory shrinkage is (a) 1/2% (b) 2% (c) 5% (d) 10%

9. Who can effectively fight crime? (a) Business associations (b) Community groups (c) Individual businessmen

Answers

1. (c) Crime currently cost all businesses an estimated $50 Billion. This estimate includes costs due to shoplifting, employee theft, arson, burglary, robbery, bad checks, bad credit and fraud, and also money spent for preventive measures.

2. (d) Employees are stealing from business at an increasing rate. Professional security personnel estimate that 8% to 9% of all employees steal on a regular basis. How long can any business survive with merchandise going out legitimately through the front door and illegitimately through the back door?

3. (b) Retail businesses currently have lost an estimated $30 Billion. The nearest rival was wholesaling. This is not an enviable position in which to be classified as #1.

4. (c) Business is estimated to spend many billions of dollars in loss prevention efforts. It is obvious the money most businesses are spending is not sufficient as the crime losses continue to escalate. These costs include guards, various types of alarms, closed circuit TV, a variety of locks, and other techniques.

5. (c) If the cost of crime was apportioned out to each adult American, $600 would have to be taken from his or her pocket. This amount does not include the added costs from increased prices caused by crime losses.

6. (c) It is startling to see how well crime does, and also ludicrous when we consider that we cannot be more effective in controlling it.

7. (d) No longer can any individual or business feel safe from the threat of burglary. A good approach is "lockup or lose It."

8. (b) Although none of these levels are very good from a profit viewpoint, a practical goal is 2 %. However, if this percentage is approximately your level at this time, you should try to improve it – resting on your laurels may put you out of business.

9. (c) Everyone can and should make an effort to reduce crime. Through individual and collectative actions, crime can be controlled and made unprofitable for the thief.

3.0 CRIME AWARENESS CHECKLIST

Answer all questions yes or no.

1. Is security considered an important management objective?

2. Does your business maintain a policy of strict enforcement and prosecution for any crime?

3. Are employees urged to discuss security problems with you?

4. Does your business have an inventory loss or "shrinkage" greater than 2%?

5. Does your business conduct background investigations of potential employees prior to employment?

6. Are your computer operations included in your security procedures?

7. Does your business maintain a standard check-cashing procedure?

8. Do employees receive updated security procedures on a regular basis?

9. Does your business have random inventories of the merchandise and/or supplies and cash audits?

10. Does your business maintain good security control of the premises?

ANSWERS

Hopefully you were able to answer yes to all questions except #4.

8–10   Correct answers indicates high management awareness, including being well informed of the problems and solutions.

6–7   Moderate awareness, management should be better informed.

4–5   Average awareness
       3 or less. Look out, your security program needs re-evaluation.

4.0   EMPLOYEE THEFT CHECKLIST AND GUIDELINES

Employee theft has been described as internal theft, embezzlement, pilferage, inventory shrinkage, and stealing. Despite the selection of any name to describe this type of theft the fact is not changed that at least 50 % of your crime-related losses are caused by your employees. Also, employee theft is growing to the extent that it is the most critical crime problem facing business today. A study indicates that as many as one in three employees admit they committed some form of theft. One in ten employees indicated they had taken property or money.

There is little evidence as why employees steal from their employers. The available research indicates that indirect factors influenced by economic need, a desire to own something, and drug addiction are involved in some cases. An important consideration is an employee who considers that what he/she is taking is not illegal or that he/she deserves it, or there may be a lack of loyalty to the company, dissatisfaction with the job, or a feeling that job security is not available. Of course, in this intangible area, there are other factors or combination of factors that may be a consideration.

Although the reasons for employee theft may result, in part, from factors beyond your control, the extent of employee theft in any business is also a reflection of its management. Generally, the more mismanagement that exists, the greater will be the theft.

Many times, the direct question arises in the employee mind, "Can I take this item and get away with it?" In many instances the question is answered almost unconsciously. Items are picked up for their own use. They may slip a small hand tool in their pocket, pick up a handful of nuts and bolts, take some electrical parts for a repair job at home, or select pencils, pens, and paper for home use. Not all employees pilfer these small items. Some carry off many hundreds and thousands of dollars worth of equipment and materials. Another reason for this pilferage is misplaced trust. In many cases, the owner and/or manager of a small business considers himself/herself close to the employees. The employee is looked to as an important and intregal part of the business. As a result the employee is trusted with keys and combinations to the doors and safes and access to money and records. Unfortunately, this employee may consider himself/herself as having the right to take whatever he/she wishes and the business develops an unwanted partner in the fact that items of value and/or money disappear. Unless you are taking the proper steps to avoid these losses which are probably occurring at this time you will lose your profit and then your business in small increments.

One of the first steps to prevent these losses is to examine the trust that has been placed in the employees. As indicated above, is the trust based on close friendship? Or, is it trust that is built on a system of accountability that reduces the opportunity for theft?

While looking at the reasons for employee theft, we know that it is an area that has much speculation and very little specific fact. If we look at the best information that is available, there are many ideas that have been given as the result of numerous studies that have been made. The following reasons have been developed for employee theft and are included here for your consideration.

In addition to the reasons given above, employees steal money and valuable property because of economic conditions. These conditions may include concern over family problems and overall local financial conditions. They may also be concerned with the security of their position and may be afraid of job loss.

Employees steal when the conditions permit them to steal. In this instance, managers are more likely to take advantage of their position because they have the ability to circumvent security systems.

Employees steal when they have access to money and valuable property. In retail stores, theft is reported more often among the people who have easier access to material items. These people include buyers, managers, cashiers, people who bag merchandise, maintenance, and food service workers. In manufacturing areas, the higher rates of theft were among the engineers, technicians, maintenance personnel, and freight handlers. In many cases, employees steal when they are part-time workers and are at a younger age. One of the studies indicates that a larger portion of the thefts are by persons 18 to 20 years of age. The speculation is that these people have fewer personal ties to the business, they are less likely to have career considerations, and are therefore less concerned with the permanency of their current position.

Employees may steal because they have a problem described as "once a thief, alway a thief." There are many theories applied to this aspect of employee stealing. The most practical approach to this situation is to avoid hiring the person who fits this category. This advice is based on the assumption that you can always determine which potential employee is the thief; certainly not an easy task. This book offers some suggestions within the available information, and is based on practical limitations, as to not hiring this type of person by the use of preemployment screening. However, there are problems that may be associated with this approach as discussed on page 23.

5.0 IS THERE AN ATTITUDE FOR DISHONESTY?

In addition to misplaced trust, does management create an attitude in which dishonesty becomes a way of life? Potential thieves are deterred if they know that strict accounting and inventory control procedures are in use to prevent employee theft. Obviously, if you were to remove these procedures then the path would be open for greater theft. What happens if the manager's brother-in-law helps himself in the stockroom without signing for the items that he takes? What happens if a supervisor is observed removing items for his personal use at home? Similarly, if strict control is not maintained with invoices, purchase orders, shipments, and returned items there would be, within a short time, an increase in the company inventory shrinkage as the employees see that accounting and inventory controls are not strict. The idea of strict controls must be reenforced on a regular basis. The use of proper stock controls, security checks, changes of key and combination locks, testing of alarms, and audits of the accounting systems and security procedures will help to show the employees that management is not lax.

Although you may be aware of the fact that physical security is an important area for loss, it is important that you implement the proper controls for physical security. For example, stock items have been lowered out of windows to confederates waiting outside. Materials, supplies, and finished parts have been carried out open doors. A building used for retail or wholesale operations, or manufacturing purposes, should have a minimum number of easily opened doors with a security guard or supervisor stationed there whenever a door is opened. This precaution is very important if unfinished materials are received, finished products are being shipped, and trash is removed.

A part of physical security is the installation of a suitable alarm system for after-hours operation to record door openings and closings.
These records are very important in the event that an explanation of particular employee movements and behavior, associated with door openings and closings, is required at a future date.

Other physical security includes discrete employee tests such as watching for the employee who is removing items after hours. The alarm system may be put out of commission and/or the doors may be used with locks that do not require opening with a key from the inside.

Use of a programmed and/or spontaneous audit is another loss prevention control that is helpful. All controls and procedures must be tested at various unexpected intervals to prevent breakdown of the controls and procedures. One technique is the use of deliberate errors injected into the system to see what the response will be. What will the employees do if more items are delivered to the shipping or receiving platform than are required on the accompanying paperwork? Will the excess items be noted and returned to stock? Will the excess stock be retained by the employee for personal use? Will it be given to the carrier for removal and division with the employee at a later time? Will the error pass unnoticed and the stock be lost because of inefficiency?

When unannounced management inspections are used as a method of control the inspections can be accomplished on a random basis during all shifts; particularly during overtime and later shifts. The shipping area is an important area for unannounced inspections.

In the record-keeping operations, the bookkeeper, accounts receivable, and accounts payable can be tested by withholding one invoice from each department or particular person and noting the reaction. Will the invoice be missed and reported to the proper management level?

The companies with the lowest rate of employee theft are the companies with a clear commitment from the top executives to the lowest level of supervisors that theft will not be tolerated. The supervisors, in turn, convey the same information to the employees.

Another important management effort should be directed to the employees understanding that their loyalty to the company will directly affect their job security and salary. The most successful loss-prevention programs have the employees realizing that it is in their best interest to discourage theft and to report any stealing by other employees. The company policies that describe exactly what practices are acceptable and not acceptable should be frequently reviewed with the employees. Also, the punishment for practices that are not acceptable should be made equally clear.

In the final analysis, you must realize that your management attitude is the most important factor in the security of the business. You should never underestimate your influence on the employees. The use of good controls, loss-prevention procedures, and security devices are important. Unfortunately, all of these efforts are wasted if you do not show personal integrity and that dishonesty will not be permitted. The physical controls can be overcome by clever employees, but your personal high standards cannot be overcome and will influence the employees.

Ask Yourself

— Do you make a real effort to screen out security risks before they are hired?
— Do you know the areas of your business where the employees have the most opportunity to steal from you?
— Do you know when they steal from you and what methods are used?
— Does your business structure encourage employees to report suspicious occurrences?
— Do you follow up on the legal aspects of the crimes and prosecute employees who are caught stealing from you?

Every employer has the requirement to reduce the losses in his business as much as possible. However, you should not create a police state in the process of reducing the losses. This effort does not require excessively large monetary expenditures. You can use preemployment screening, operational controls, and a policy of open, useful communication with employees.

Hiring Honest Employees

The best method to stop employee theft is simply not to hire those employees who are inclined to steal. Unfortunately, this method is also impossible to accomplish. You must set up a screening process that will remove the obvious security risks. Many experts believe that preemployment personnel screening is the most important safeguard against internal theft. However, some of the studies that have been completed indicate that employers are moving away from preemployment screenings and using stricter job controls. No doubt that, in selected businesses where the loss potential is high, management is using a combination of the two techniques. One of the problems related to preemployment screening is the fact of legal restrictions covering what you may and may not ask the prospective employee. Also, the employee's prior company may refuse to provide information describing their past employee.

Some Basic Guidelines for You

— Always have the applicant complete a written application and interview the applicant. Be sure that your written application does not discriminate against particular persons as specified by state and federal law. Your attorney can advise you as to the applicable state and federal requirements. Be certain to have your attorney review your application form before it is put into use.

— Try to avoid hiring prospects with criminal convictions on their record. This suggestion is not meant to be a steadfast rule because individual judgments must be made as to the degree of rehabilitation that has occurred and what crime was committed. Be aware of the fact that it is **illegal to ask** for information about arrest records that did not lead to convictions.

— When requesting references, which is a very important part of the procedure, keep in mind that persons who are contacted will usually give favorable opinions. Ask these primary references for secondary references that you may contact. In contacting the latter, make it clear to these persons that the applicant did not refer you to them.

— During the interview be certain to assess the applicant's maturity and values. Observe any gestures that are made and consider them with the spoken comments. Keep detailed records of the questions, answers, and your observations during the interview.

— Use the available psychological deterrents. Inform the applicant that your business routinely runs a security check on the background of each new applicant and/or that a bonding application must be filled out. The hope is that potentially dishonest employees will not go beyond their initial application.

— Obtain a credit bureau report on the potential employee, making certain that you follow the guidelines established by state and federal requirements and reviewed by your attorney as to the methods used to obtain the information.

6.0   AREAS, METHODS, AND CONTROLS

There is documentation indicating that cases of employee theft have been discovered in almost every conceivable phase of business operations, from theft of petty cash to railroad cars. A careful review of the theft records that are available indicates there is an infinite number of areas in which theft can occur and that many methods are used.

Areas That are Most Vulnerable

— Shipping and receiving departments
— Inventory records
— General accounting and associated record keeping
— Cash sales
— Accounts payable
— Accounts receivable
— Payroll funds and records
— Employee purchases

Some Methods of Theft

— Giving free merchandise to friends and relatives
— Aiding shoplifting friends by creating situations for easy theft
— Theft from a cash register
— Issuance of false refunds for merchandise
— Use of back door to take out merchandise
— Alteration of cash register records
— Avoidance of package examination and control
— Embezzlement
— Check forgery
— Theft of merchandise and/or parts from service department
— Creation of false markdowns on sales tags
— Stealing credit cards
— Manipulating computers and systems
— Thefts by night cleaning crew
— Use of duplicate keys to doors
— Theft of computer time

This short list indicates some of the methods that exist for employees to exploit the many opportunities for theft.

Some Methods of Control

The following are opportunities for your control by using proper procedures:

— Use random spot checks of all phases of your business.
— Constantly use audits covering all areas of the business.

— Examine the payroll records to be certain that you are not paying a salary to a fictitious or dead employee.

— Be certain that physical inventory procedures are completed in detail and the records should be carefully analyzed.

— Maintain complete records of your physical equipment and stock and be able to identify them during an audit.

— Examine all incoming and outgoing shipments against purchase orders and invoices.

— Lock all supply and storage rooms and allow access to them only under proper supervision.

— Provide cross-checking of all activities to eliminate the possibility that one employee has complete control of any one operation from the beginning to the end.

— All documents, particularly checks, should have serial numbers and a complete name and address of your business on them. These numbered checks should be used to make all payments including the payroll.

— Limit access to specific employees to restricted areas with the use of keys or identification cards. There are new and more sophisticated technologies available that use voice and fingerprints for controlled access to specific areas, replacing the use of identification cards and badges.

— When cellular telephones are used for internal and external communications you must avoid security leaks, unauthorized calls, and improper charges. Use a cellular service that provides scrambled telephone signals and/or requires the use of a Personal Identification Number (PIN) for maximum security and control. Ask your local cellular telephone system management for their suggestions.

7.0   ALARM AND SECURITY SYSTEMS

An alarm and security system is intended to provide a warning of man-made or climatic events that may damage the premises and/or an intruder(s) who plans to burglarize your premises. A typical system includes an assembly of equipment that provides the indication of a problem. In addition to the problem of the intent by a person(s) to steal money, products, or damage the facilities there may be damage caused by fire or some external weather condition such as a flood or earthquake. The problem may also be nonhuman-related with a dangerous condition caused by an internal operational system change such as an alteration in a chemical process, excess heat in an area, lack of fuel to maintain a particular operation, failure of a heating system, and many other situations.

An alarm and security system has three basic parts regardless of the type of system. These parts work in sequence with each other as a chain reaction.

Sensor: This device responses to a physical, audio, or electronic stimulus such as heat, light, sound, pressure, motion, or other indicator.

Circuit: A system, usually electrical, that receives the information from the sensor indicating that a stimulus was received by the sensor.

Signal: The circuit activates a signal to indicate the fact that the sensor has responded to a stimulus. The signal can be in many forms such as a light, bell, reading on a metering device, computer system, or automatic message to an external location such as the police and fire departments.

An alarm system has it benefits and its drawbacks. From a security standpoint it indicates that a person(s)—or in some cases animal(s)— has attempted or has gained entry at a specific location. An external signal resulting from an alarm may be useful in frightening any intruder and causing the intruder to leave. If an internal signal is used it will provide a warning to you as to what has occurred without warning the intruder and you may take the proper response. In either case the drawback for an alarm system is that it does not operate by itself to apprehend the intruder and should not be considered as a sufficient stand-alone protection system except in situations where only minimal protection is required.

Before making a committment to install an alarm system, a decision must be made as to what is to be protected and what is the adequate type of system to properly do the job. You must also consider the cost of the protection against the value of what is to be protected. Among the numerous factors to be considered is the type of system, such as a Central Station located within the premises, and whether it will provide audible internal warnings and/or be connected to the local police and fire departments. Will the system use silent remote alarms that provide indications within the company and/or is connected to the local police and fire department?

The selection of the equipment that will comprise the chosen type of system should be done with the help of a local professional alarm and security company that will be responsible for the actual installation. The type of equipment that is available is extensive and is constantly being improved and expanded. The professional people at the alarm and security company will be able to assist you in your choices. The selection of personnel to be a part of the alarm system also requires your thought and professional advice. You will have to consider the use of existing and/or additional employees or the use of professional security personnel. The size of your company, what you have to protect, and your budget are all important factors that you must consider.

Security

In retail business, the cash register and/or point of sale computer terminals with a built-in cash drawer(s) are an open invitation for employee theft. Some of the safeguards that can be used include:

— Assign each cashier the use of only one cash drawer for easier accounting of losses.

— Each sale should be entered into the cash register in sequence and a receipt must be given to the customer for each sale.

—A supervisor must sign for each void or overcharge correction in excess of a specific amount of money. Excessive voids, overcharges, and refunds may indicate an employee problem.

—Maintain each cash register in proper operating condition with the internal detail tapes to prevent losses from sales that are not properly recorded by the cashier.

—Use unannounced testing to prevent unauthorized changing of prices at the cash register and have professional shoppers make purchases to see if proper cash register procedures are used.

Commercial security alarm systems are designed to prevent employee and customer theft and burglaries. In retail stores the system(s) also helps to prevent holdups. A combination of video cameras, audio recording systems, and electronic security devices including door contacts, motion detectors, glass breakage sensors, portable and permanently installed holdup signaling devices, temperature sensors, smoke detectors, and heat detectors are used. Any combination of components can be included in a system(s) that is designed for your particular requirements.

In various wholesale and distributor locations, the video cameras, sensors, and time-lapse film recorders will monitor the traffic in and out of doors, loading and unloading facilities, and ground level windows. Depending on the type of system(s) installed there is instant viewing of the events on video monitors and simultaneous permanent recording in time-lapse film recorders.

In retail stores, the video cameras will record any specific areas where merchandise is displayed and the sale at the cash register. Customer response is shown on a video monitor and simultaneously in a time-lapse film recorder. This viewing and recording will discourage any of the theft practices of merchandise and improprieties at the cash register.

An appropriate response to any of these systems in the event of a problem can be through internal management and/or local police.

An important factor that you must consider in planning an installation of a covert surveillance system is to understand the ethical and legal issues involved in the use of these systems. Large and small companies find covert cameras and audio recording equipment very useful to enable managers to watch customers and employees—particularly when the managers are not located in the immediate area— without the people knowing they are being watched. Management must realize there are legal safeguards in many states where this equipment cannot be used without proper notification of the people involved. Discovery of the covert equipment by the employees can have ramifications such as a devastating effect on morale. This situation will adversely affect the quality and quantity of work that is accomplished. Before any covert surveillance system is installed you should review the potential ethical and legal issues with your attorney and the provider of the equipment to avoid any problems.

The technology involved in covert surveillance systems has been improved in quality and miniaturization during recent years to the extent that cameras and recording equipment can be hidden in such unusual places as wall pictures, radios, pencil sharpeners, mirrors, clocks, smoke detectors, exit signs, emergency lights, books, and a wide variety of other discreet places. We have reached a point in the technology where imagination as to location, with due consideration of cost, is the only limiting factor for installation of this equipment.

8.0   THE EFFECTIVE METHODS THAT YOU CAN USE

The most effective method to reduce theft in retail businesses has been to apprehend the person(s) involved in a theft, terminate his/her employment, and advise the other employees of the situation. This procedure will also reduce overall employee theft by giving the other employees a clear example of what may happen to them. The additional step of prosecuting the offender is also an important factor in reducing overall employee theft.

Prosecuting an employee is also important when the employee has only been a minor part of an overall conspiracy of a group of employees. There may have been a large number of people stealing merchandise or helping a shoplifter(s). Unless you are willing to consider special circumstances for a particular employee, all of the employees involved must be treated alike. If you consider special circumstances for one employee you should advise all of the employees as to your actions.

9.0   VIOLENCE AS A RESULT OF PROSECUTION

Although violence in the workplace is not theft, it can be related to theft. Angry workers or spouses may attack other employees within the company premises and/or damage the company premises in retaliation for theft prosecution and dismissal. Unfortunately, this type of violence has been increasing. To help in avoiding the angry worker problem extreme care must be used in the preemployment personal background check, where you should be looking for potential persons who may react in this manner. Also, you must be careful that all of your screening and investigations are accomplished within the existing laws. To also help in avoiding the angry employee/spouse problem you must also have proper security at the entrance to your facility to prevent their entrance into your facility. Your local police department, your own security system, and your attorney can work together to help prevent this type of violence.

Until now, these methods have apparently not been as effective in manufacturing businesses. Perhaps the current lower rate of prosecution for this problem area is based on the fact that these businesses have not been willing to expose the problem to public view. This reluctance to publicly prosecute an offender may be the cause of the lower effectivness.

With more extensive communication of business policy on employee theft and a detail explanation of the consequences resulting from a theft there is a definite reduction of employee theft. When employees understand exactly what the business policy is, they must weigh the consequences against any action that they may be considering.

Co-Worker Attitudes

Among the employees, the consideration of co-workers' attitudes affects employee theft. The results found in a few of the studies that have been completed indicate that if the co-worker(s) encourages theft or does nothing to discourage a theft the effect is to create the likelihood of a theft occurring. If the co-worker acts to discourage a theft, or threatens to inform management this action will be a greater deterrent to a theft than the statement of prosecution indicated in the business policy published by management.

10.0 DEFINING THEFT FOR YOUR EMPLOYEES

There must be a clear definition of what is considered to be employee theft and what is not theft. The business policy published by management may state that all theft is considered wrong and will be punished. In practice, will the taking of a few pens or pencils and a small quantity of paper for personal use be considered in the same category as taking money from the cash register or removing merchandise from stock? It is easy to say that all of these actions are theft and should be treated as such. However, in a practical consideration of this important problem and your relationship with your employees you must establish the guidelines that you will use.

You must also determine a practical value for theft that you consider important for your business. This value in dollars is the amount that you say is worth the expense of arresting, discharging, and prosecuting an employee. Also, in your calculation you must consider the fact that many small thefts added together can be dangerous to your business. These decisions are very important to the success of your antitheft efforts.

Auditing and Inventory Controls reduce pilferage, embezzlement, and the resulting high costs of theft to your business through the use of internal controls. These audits should be done on a regular semiannual and annual cycle. Also, unannounced audits can also be very revealing as they prevent the hiding of the employee theft based on the knowledge of the precise time schedule for an audit.

An important consideration is to inform the employees of the facts as you see them. Advise each employee as to the cost to them for employee theft. As an example, there will be less money available for salary increases, more jobs will be lost if the business is unable to operate in a profitable condition, and in extreme cases, the business may have to close down.

11.0   EMPLOYEE PRIVACY IS A SECURITY DILEMMA

A problem for business management is how to protect the business from employee theft and maintain the employee's right to privacy. A great deal of time has been spent in the study of this problem at the state and federal government levels. Congress has been working on various aspects of employee rights and how to protect them in many types of businesses. Some businesses have been accused of violating employee rights by using wiretapping and eavesdropping devices. However, the person(s) responsible for the security of the business and reducing employee theft losses must be able to use the latest technology to perform the job.

Electronic monitoring in the computer age is more sophisticated than the older forms of surveillance or investigation which included rummaging through a person's desk or file cabinet. Closed circuit television, access to files on a computer, and telephone monitoring equipment have made watching employee actions much easier. Such activity has made rights advocacy groups complain that employees have their right to privacy that must be balanced against the security needs of the employer.

The most important step for any business management is to contact their attorney before implementing any security measures to oversee their employees to be certain that what they are planning to do meets the current federal and state legal requirements.

12.0 EXTERNAL TELEPHONE HOTLINE SERVICE

Sometimes a business will consider the use of incentives—usually financial—as a means to encourage employees to report theft. Some management consider this technique to be a very important tool. Other management consider this technique as a means to hurt employee morale. A variation of this direct reporting system is to provide an external telephone hotline service where employees can call anonymously to an outside source to report internal theft. There are companies that provide this service. Interestingly, in a number of instances where this system has been used, the employees are not interested in a financial reward or they consider it as a secondary interest. The anonymity is the important factor. Again, contact your attorney before implementing any reporting system to be certain of your legal position.

Criminal Description Information

Physical Description

HEIGHT_____

WEIGHT_____

NATIONALITY (IF KNOWN)_____

COMPLEXION_____

EYES — COLOR — EYEGLASSES
(ALERT — NORMAL — DROOPY)
_____

VISIBLE SCARS, MARKS, TATTOOS
_____

AGE_____

Method of Escape

DIRECTION_____

LICENSE_____

VEHICLE DESCRIPTION_____
_____

Remarks_____
_____
_____

IN EMERGENCY
CALL POLICE IMMEDIATELY

HAT

HAIR   COLOR - CUT

BEARD OR MOUSTACHE
SIDEBURNS

SHIRT

NECKTIE

JACKET
OR
COAT

WEAPON

RIGHT
OR
LEFT
HANDED

TROUSERS

SHOES

13.0   IDEAS FOR YOUR IMMEDIATE USE

While you are considering the implementation of any of the activities described on page 43, there are a number of tested ideas that you may put to use in reducing potential losses.

— Do not allow one employee to manage or perform all merchandising functions.

— Separate the receiving, purchasing, accounts receivable, and accounts payable duties.

— Separate the accounting process from the cash handling operations.

— Maintain management control of all payment authorizations.

— Keep blank checks under lock and key. Do not presign or use uncoded and unnumbered checks.

— Be certain to reconcile each cancelled check with the original invoice or voucher that was paid.

— Maintain secure exits and wherever possible restrict employees to one exit. Prevent the use of any exit at the rear of the business premises except as authorized by management.

— Establish strict package controls and inspect every package that leaves the premises. Do not allow exceptions to this rule.

— Require a total of cash register receipts **daily and inspect** each tape for unusual transactions. Each sales person must be identified on each slip. The money from each cash register must be deposited daily. Use professional shoppers, posing as customers, to test the integrity of the clerks. Simplify the red tape, eliminate useless procedures, and make it more difficult for an employee to disguise any theft.

14.0 COMPUTER SYSTEMS

Computers and computer systems have become an integral part of every business. Companies have given many of the details pertaining to their management financial matters, management and operational functions, and controls to this high-tech equipment and gained much in their capabilities to function at a faster pace and have more control over their operations. Unfortunately, there is a downside to this advancement, much of the valuable confidential company information is exposed to internal and external theft. The potential danger is based on the fact that concentration of a huge amount of vital information, equivalent to hundreds of document pages, is easily transported on small portable computer disks. These disks can be carried out of the office with almost no effort.

Another potential danger to vital information is the fact that it can be sent, electronically, to other computers outside the company within fractions of a second. Unless proper programming efforts are used the loss of this information will go undetected.

Proper programming efforts are also required to protect the company information in the computers from outside intrusion. Unless proper precautions are established, people knowledgeable with computer operations and having the proper equipment can enter the company computers from external sites to obtain confidential information and create problems with the operation of the company computers.

Some of the common problems include:

The addition of programming instructions, by programmers, within existing programs to destroy data, issue payroll checks to nonexistent employees, issue checks to fictitious invoices, and create errors that cause downtime and expenses for the company. Other personnel may alter computer records to hide the theft of inventory items and company equipment.

The unauthorized use of computer time involves playing computer games and conducting personal business using the company computer system.

Most computer crimes can be prevented when management understands the potential problems and what should be done to prevent the occurrence of the crimes. A computer security system should be implemented prior to the installation of any computer system. The proper time to implement the security system is at the planning stage for the initial installation of a computer system and/or the changeover from the existing system to the new computer system.

A security policy that is considered the central part of the computer system is very important. It should include the following items:

No computer system is better than the people involved in it. One method to be certain the people will adhere to company policy is to do a thorough background check on the people before they become part of the computer system operation. On a day-to-day basis, only the people directly involved with the operation of the computer system should be permitted in the area where the computer equipment is located. If repair personnel and other technical experts are required in the computer area they must be thoroughly screened and their identification verified before they are permitted to enter the area. A company supervisor should be available with the noncompany personnel when they are in the computer area.

Computer areas should be isolated, with a minimum of windows and doors. The windows should be secure to prevent entrance. Each door should be kept closed and secured. Entrance should be, by passing a security guard and/or an electronic system that requires a special card entered into a lock. Many companies use a photo-identification card, fingerprint identification, or special code system that identifies the person as an employee or noncompany personnel with the proper need-to-know requirement to enter the computer area.

Other important precautions include a physical separation of the management for the computer system and the employees that have access to it. Personnel should be rotated on a regular basis so that no one person, or group of people, has constant control and access to the computer system and area.

The output of your computer system must be guarded with the same care as the physical equipment and the access to it. You have to be concerned with the output of the system which may be on a monitor screen and/or printed on computer paper or a computer disk. Careful records must be kept as to who uses the computer system—date and time—and what is done with the physical output items. The disposition of each computer printout and disk must be carefully logged into a record to permit accounting for each item. Audits most be performed at least once each year to be certain the records are properly maintained and are accurate.

Remember one important bit of advice. The security system will not function properly unless the people in it are willing to devote the effort to maintain and use it. You, as the management of the company, must instill in your employees the concept that it is important for the employees to properly maintain the security system.

15.0 IMPROVED COMMUNICATIONS WILL HELP YOU

The leadership shown by management must be firm and reasonable.

The following management practices have been proven to be helpful in developing better communications between employees and management:

— Most of the employees will use their personal ethical training to follow good examples. Therefore, management must provide these examples.

— Train new employees by advising them of your requirements and the standards by which they will be expected to perform. Explain all the security procedures and stress their importance. Emphasize the fact that any deviations will be thoroughly investigated and treated according to established company policy.

— Establish a grievance and/or suggestion procedure and give the employees an outlet for disagreement with management. Management must be receptive to all grievances and suggestions that are submitted. All employees should be aware of the procedures' existence and they must be certain that no reprisals will be taken against any employee who uses the grievance and suggestion procedure.

— Use a review system for periodic evaluation of each employee's performance and encourage them to evaluate management. Unrealistic performance standards imposed on an employee will lead to desperation or anger. This situation may result in dishonesty and/or a "get even" attitude. A periodic review of salaries, wages, and benefits will help to eliminate some of the feelings that may force employees to steal from the business.

— Delegate some of the business responsibility. Unless there is decision-making among all levels of employees, there is a tendency for an "It's us against them!" attitude to develop. Delegate some aspects of the business accountability to a few of the employees as no decision is valid if it is lost in a "buck passing" routine.

— Advise the employees as to the risks of dishonesty in the business. Fear of apprehension and prosecution is often an excellent deterrent to a crime. When the threat of jail exists, there is a good chance the employee will think twice before committing a crime. Report all criminal acts to the proper authorities and cooperate with them. Prosecution is admittedly expensive and slow; however, if employee theft is to be reduced, dishonest employees must be prosecuted to the fullest extent of the law. Be certain that all employees are aware of any criminal acts that occur and the resulting actions that are taken by management and the law authorities.

— Develop a bonus or incentive plan for the employees. If all losses are less than a prescribed amount per year,

half-year, quarter-year, or any other time base the employees will share in a bonus based on the savings. This type of
payment can be very successful in creating a "reduce-the-
losses" attitude.

16.0 BAD CHECKS AND CREDIT CARD LOSSES

With 90% of the business volume in the U.S. accomplished by checks, there are more than 63 billion checks written on 200 million checking accounts at the 22,000 financial institutions that are in operation. In addition, more than one-half of all retail transactions are conducted with credit cards. More than 2.0 billion retail transactions are anticipated in the year 2000.

The magnitude of these transactions indicates that potential losses due to the misuse of checks and credit cards are enormous and present a serious problem to any business. There are, in essence, two approaches to the solution of the problem. One approach is as an individual business and the second approach is collective as a community of businesses. The recommendation is that the two approaches be combined.

What the Individual Business Should Do—Use a Business Policy

The easiest solution is to stop accepting payments in the form of checks and credit cards. However, in view of the competitive nature of the marketplace and the importance of service, this solution is, of course, impossible. The practical approach is to establish a business policy that reduces loss as much as possible while maintaining the status and growth of the business. The following are basic rules for cashing checks that *any* policy should cover:

Not Acceptable Check Cashing

— Cash checks without a minimum of two proper forms of identification as defined for the requirements of your business.
— Cash checks for a sum of money that is larger than the purchase that has been made.
— Accept out-of-the-area checks.
— Accept checks that are not imprinted with the name and address of the person involved in the transaction.
— Accept post or past-dated checks.
— Accept payroll (especially government) checks without the proper identification.
— Accept certified or cashier's checks without proper identification.
— Accept checks with any alterations.
— Accept credit cards without referring to the latest delinquent list.

Acceptable Check Cashing

— Always verify the signature on all identification items presented with the check. If there is the slightest doubt as to the validity of the signatures, then reject the check. Refer to the two illustrations of a check showing the important features to be examined when a check is presented for payment.

We know that using false identification is a major factor contributing to the losses resulting from checks and credit cards. Each business should define the acceptable and unacceptable identification procedures that pertain to their operations. The following procedures are some of the more common types usually included in both categories.

Acceptable Identification

— Valid driver's license issued by the state in which the business is located.
— Bank and organization type credit cards.
— National retail business credit cards.
— Employee identification cards issued by reputable companies showing the employee's photograph.

Not Acceptable Identification

— Social Security cards.
— Gasoline company credit cards.
— Library membership cards.
— Membership cards issued by various local and national social organizations.

Additional Procedures You Can Use

There are a number of other procedures that can be used to enhance the existing identification techniques used in a business. The selection of one or more of these additional procedures depends on the type of business, the extent of the identification techniques currently in use, and the costs required to begin any of these additional procedures.

Camera systems that photograph the person cashing the check with the identification card(s) and the check. The film is only developed when a bad check is returned and the check is sent to the writer for collection.

Dry thumb print system that permits the recording of the thumb print of the check writer as an aid in apprehension of bad check passers.

Computer systems that permit instant online verification of the person and the check. Specific airlines and major bank card organizations utilize these systems.

An individual identification card issued by your business. The employees must examine the card when a check is presented.

Important features to be examined
when a check is presented for payment

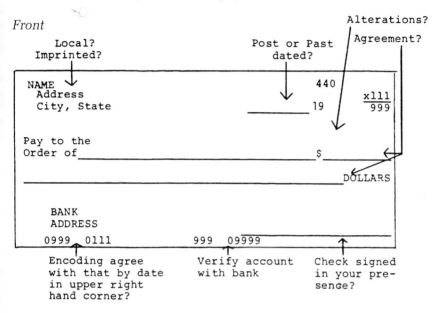

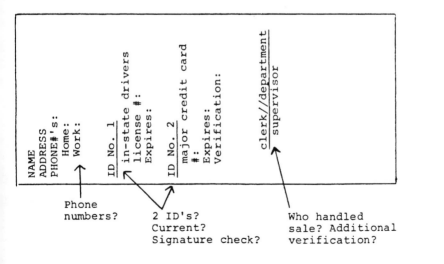

17.0 WHAT THE COMMUNITY BUSINESSES SHOULD DO

A communication system should be used to alert neighboring businesses of a person who is passing bad checks or using a stolen credit card. This helps the other businesses who are potential victims to be on the alert.

Cooperate with local, state, and federal law enforcement authorities by reporting the bogus checks, false identification cards, and stolen credit cards.

Publicize Your Business Policy

One of the best deterrents for business crime is a widespread knowledge of your policies related to cashing checks and accepting credit cards.

Post your business policy in prominent locations where the statements will alert all your customers.

Train all the employees by discussing your business policy and stress the fact that no exceptions are permitted. Be certain to alert them as to the methods and techniques that are used by persons passing bad checks and using stolen credit cards.

Develop a reference source for examining checks that is easy to use by your employees. Refer to the illustration of a check included on page 59.

Stress the importance of your check and credit card policy. Some businesses consider a successful deterrent is to make the employees who deviate from the policy responsible for the resulting losses.

18.0 WHEN THE COMMUNITY BUSINESSES WORK TOGETHER

The individual business can adapt any of these, or other suitable procedures, to reduce its losses from the actions of the people who intend to defraud using bad checks and the improper use of credit cards. However, there are problems related to these procedures when considered by the consumers who are the customers of the individual business.

Most customers have two viewpoints pertaining to these procedures. They usually understand the business problems that cause the need for these procedures to be used. However, they are resentful of the time and effort that are required of them when they are customers of the business. Many will see these procedures as an imposition on them, an unnecessary use of their time, and a questioning of their personal integrity. They may carry these thoughts to the extreme of not patronizing a particular business, preferring to go to another business where there are less restrictions and requirements on them.

In order to overcome these customer problems, businesses in many communities have benefited by joining together in one association for common action. The business managements have established community standards to reduce their losses and maintain good customer relations. The results have produced a number of important benefits to each business:

— The volume of bad checks and instances of improper use of credit cards have been reduced significantly.

— Results have been attributed to the same or similar procedures being used by each business and the deterrent provided by the general public's knowledge that the particular business community is strict in its financial operations.

— With the enforcement of the same procedures by all the businesses in one community the customers will not consider any individual business as performing an imposition on them or questioning their personal integrity.

19.0 BUSINESS ASSOCIATIONS THAT CAN HELP YOU

The coordination of the business managements into an effective community group is easier to accomplish through an existing business association, such as a local Chamber of Commerce, Better Business Bureau, or Merchants Association. There are many advantages to the use of an existing association. The names of all the businesses that should be a part of the activity are on record and contact with these businesses exists through one location. The need for new office space and other similar expenses can be avoided. The authority of the existing association is established in the community. Shopping malls and other groups of businesses can also join with any of these established associations for this effort without losing their individuality for any other planned activities.

Another benefit to the use of an existing association is the fact that most consumers will have at least a minimum understanding of the prior efforts by the association as a business and consumer advocate. Any advertising campaign that is created to alert customers to the planned effort of fraud reduction will be more easily accepted when given the endorsement of the association. The result will be much less consumer resistance.

The following "CRIMINAL DESCRIPTION INFORMA-TION" is useful to help employees in remembering the **important features** of the individual(s) that are part of any suspicious business transaction or crime. This information should be communicated to the police and all community groups and associations.

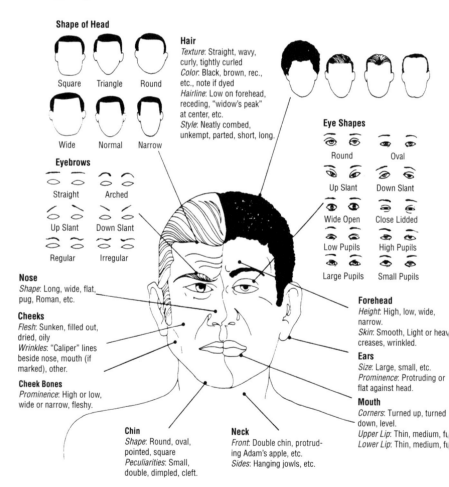

20.0 TRADE ASSOCIATIONS

The following trade associations are only a few that can be helpful to retailers interested in setting up crime-related loss reduction programs. Some associations conduct lectures or seminars on crime prevention at their annual conventions, while others make booklets, motion pictures, or other aids available. Specific *associations are engaged in gathering* statistical data on the incidence and impact of crime and representing the interests of specific industries before Federal and State government agencies.

Some of the organizations active in these areas are:

AMERICAN SOCIETY FOR INDUSTRIAL SECURITY
2000 K Street, NW
Washington, DC 20006

CHAMBER OF COMMERCE OF THE UNITED STATES
1615 H Street, NW
Washington, DC 20006

JEWELERS SECURITY ALLIANCE OF THE U.S.
535 Fifth Avenue
New York, NY 10017

MASS RETAILING INSTITUTE
570 Seventh Avenue
New York, NY 10018

MENSWEAR RETAILERS OF AMERICA
390 National Press Building
Washington, DC 20004

NATIONAL ASSOCIATION OF FOOD CHAINS
1725 I Street NW
Washington, DC 20004

NATIONAL ASSOCIATION OF RETAIL GROCERS
OF THE UNITED STATES
2000 Spring Road
Road Oak Brook, IL 60521

NATIONAL COUNCIL ON CRIME AND DELINQUENCY
Continental Plaza
411 Hackensack Avenue
Hakensack, NJ 07051

NATIONAL FEDERATION OF INDEPENDENT BUSINESS
150 West 20th Avenue
San Mateo, CA 94403

NATIONAL RETAIL MERCHANTS ASSOCIATION
100 West Street
New York, NY 10001

SUPER MARKET INSTITUTES, INC.
200 East Ontario Street
Chicago, IL 60611

Periodicals

ASSETS PROTECTION
P.O. Box 5327
Madison, WI 53705

COUNTERFORCE (Terrorism)
4039 Cole, Suite 107
Dallas, TX 25204

CRIME AND PROTECTION
324 South Beverly Drive
Suite 204
Beverly Hills, CA 90212

OCCUPATIONAL HAZARD
Industrial Publishing Co.
614 Superior Avenue
Cleveland, OH 44102

SECURITY MANAGEMENT
2000 K Street, NW
Washington, DC 20006

SECURITY SYSTEMS DIGEST AND
TRAINING AIDS DIGEST
Washington Crimes News Service
7520 Little River Turnpike
Annandale, VA 22003

SECURITY WORLD
2539 South La Cienaga Blvd.
Los Angeles, CA 90034

The reference department of your local public library can assist you in finding any other organizations that you may be interested in contacting.

21.0   LAW ENFORCEMENT AGENCIES

Your state law enforcement agencies, including the state troopers, highway patrol, etc., usually have specialists who concentrate their efforts on preventing and solving crimes against business. The police departments of most large cities have similar specialized staffs. They are often available for consultation with individual businesses and/or groups of merchants.

Retailers and other businesses can profit from a **close liaison with local law** enforcement agencies. The services available to businesspeople may vary in different areas. Generally, the services include guidance on crime prevention programs, alerting businessmen to new criminal schemes, and business-area patrols during the closing hours. In some jurisdictions, intrusion alarms are wired from the business to the local police stations. These systems permit the police to respond quickly to any problem that may occur.

22.0   STATE PLANNING AGENCIES

Several states have established a State Planning Agency to receive and administer grants from the Law Enforcement Assistance Administration for the purpose of improving state-wide law enforcement and criminal justice programs. These programs include professional training for police officers, legal guidance for city police, improvement of communications, setup or improvement of crime laboratories, drug abuse education, and court and institutional improvement. A list of the established State Planning Agencies is included below.

ALABAMA
Mr. Luke Eugene Marshal, *Chief*
Law Enforcement/Traffic Safety Division
Alabama Department of Economic
and Community Affairs
401 Adams Avenue, P.O. Box 5690
Montgomery, AL 36103-5690
Tel.: 334-242-5803 Fax: 334-242-0712

AMERICAN SAMOA

Mr. La'auli Ale Filoali'i,
Executive Director
Criminal Justice Planning Agency
American Samoa Government
P. O. Box 3760
Pago Pago, AQ 96799
Tel.: 011-684-633-4155   Fax: 011-684-633-1838

ARIZONA

Mr. Rex M. Holgerson, *Executive Director*
Arizona Criminal Justice Commission
1501 West Washington Suite 207
Phoenix, AZ 85007
Tel.: 602-542-1928 Fax: 602-542-4852

ARKANSAS

Colonel John R Bailey, *Director*
Arkansas State Police
P. O. Box 5901
Local Rock, AR 72215
Tel.: 501-221-8200 Fax: 501-224-4722

CALIFORNIA

Mr. Ray Johnson, *Executive Director*
Office of Criminal Justice Planning
1130 K Street, Suite 300
Sacramento, CA 95814
Tel.: 916-324-9140   FAX: 916-327-5673

Chief Ted J. Mertens
Manhattan Beach Police Department
420 15th Street
Manhattan Beach, CA 90266
Tel.: 310-545-5621 x 302   Fax: 310-546-7661

Mr. Michael F. Thompson, *Director*
Mayor's Criminal Justice Planning Office
City Hall, Room M-10
200 North Spring Street
Los Angeles, CA 90012
Tel.: 213-485-4425 Fax: 213-847-3004

COLORADO

Sheriff George Epp
Boulder County Sheriff's Department
1777 6th Street
Boulder, CO 80302
Tel.: 303-441-4605 Fax: 303-441-4739

Mr. William R. Woodward, *Director*
Division of Criminal Justice
Colorado Department of Public Safety
700 Kipling Street
Suite 1000
Denver, CO 80215
Tel.: 303-239-4442 Fax: 303-239-4491

CONNECTICUT

Chief John P. Ambrogio
Hamden Police Department
2900 Dixwell Avenue
Hamden, CT 06518
Tel.: 203-230-4015 Fax: 203-230-4068

Mr. Len D'Amico,
Under Secretary for Policy
Development and Planning
Office of Policy and Management
450 Capitol Avenue
Hartford, CT 06134-1441
Tel.: 860-418-6416 Fax: 860-418-6496

DELAWARE

Mr. James Kane, *Acting Director*
Criminal Justice Council
Carvel State Office Building
4th Floor
820 North French Street
Wilmington, DE 19801
Tel.: 302-577-3437 Fax: 302-577-3440

DISTRICT OF COLUMBIA

Mr. Robert L. Lester, *Director*
Office of Grants Management &
Development
717 14th Street, NW, Suite 500
Washington, DC 20005
Tel.: 202-727-6537 Fax: 202-727-1617

FLORIDA

Major Linda Loizzo
Assistant Chief of Police
North Miami Beach Police Department
16901 NE 19 Avenue
No. Miami Beach, FL 33162
Tel.: 305-787-6021 Fax: 305-948-2969

Mr. James T. Moore
Commissioner
Florida Department of
Law Enforcement
P. O. Box 1489
Tallahassee, FL 32302
Tel.: 904-487-3471 Fax: 904-488-2189

GEORGIA

Ms. Maria Gilland, *Director*
Criminal Justice Coordinating Council
503 Oak Place, Suite 540
Atlanta, GA 30349
Tel.: 404-559-4949 Fax: 404-559-4960

HAWAII

The Hon. Margery S. Bronster
Attomey General of Hawaii
Office of the Attorney General
425 Queen Street
Honolulu, HI 96813
Tel.: 808 586-1282 Fax: 808-586-1239

IDAHO

Mr. Michael C. Prentice, *Deputy Director*
Idaho Department of
Juvenile Corrections
P. O. Box 83720
Boise, ID 83720-0285
or 400 N. Tenth
Boise, ID 83702
Tel.: 208-334-5103 Fax: 208-334-5120

ILLINOIS

Mr. Mark W. Rizzo, *C.E.O.*
Freedom Flyer Ministries, Inc.
7544 S. Harlem
Bridgeview, IL 60455
Tel.: 708-594-8913

Mr. Thomas F. Baker
Executive Director
Illinois Criminal Justice
Information Authority
120 South Riverside Plaza
10th Floor
Chicago, IL 60606
Tel.: 312-793-8941 Fax: 312-793-8422

Mr. Joseph M. Claps
Chief of Criminal Justice
Office of the Attorney General
100 W. Randolph Street, 12th Floor
Chicago, IL 60601
Tel.: 312-814-5376/5377
Fax: 312-814-5024

INDIANA

Ms. Catherine O'Connor
Executive Director
Indiana Criminal Justice Institute
302 West Washington Strect
Room E209
Indianapolis, IN 46204
Tel.: 317-232-2560 Fax: 317-232-4979

IOWA

Mr. David Hudson
Administrative Assistant
Office of the Governor
State of Iowa
State Capitol
Des Moines,IA 50319
Tel.: 515-281-8318 Fax: 515-281-6611

KENTUCKY

Mr. E. Daniel Cherry
Secretary of the Justice Cabinet
Bush Building, 2nd Floor
403 Wapping Street
Frankfort, KY 40601
Tel.: 502-564-7554 Fax: 502-564-4840

J. Price Foster, *Ph.D.*
Professor, Justice Administration
University of Louisville
1631 Dunbarton Wynde
Louisville, KY 40205
Tel.: 502-852-8959/U 459-1531/H
Fax: 502-852-0065/U 852-5738/O

LOUISIANA

Mr. Michael Ranatza, *Director*
Louisiana Commission on
Law Enforcement and
Administration of Justice
1885 Woodale Boulevard, Room 708
Baton Rouge, LA 70806
Tel.: 504-925-4430/4418
FAX: 504-925-1998

MARIANA ISLANDS

Mr. Joaquin T. Ogumoro
Executive Director
Criminal Justice Planning Agency
Northern Mariana Islands
P.O.Box 1133 CK
Saipan, MP 96950
Tel.: 670-664-4550 Fax: 670-664-4560

MARYLAND

Mr. Andrew L. Sonner
State's Attorney
Montgomery County
State's Attorney Office
50 Courthouse Square, 5th Floor
Rockville, MD 20850-2320
Tel.: 301-217-7333 Fax: 301-217-7441

Mr. Thomas H. Carr, *Director*
Washington-Baltimore HIDTA
Office of National Drug Control Policy
Executive Office of the President
7500 Greenway Center Drive
Greenbelt, MD 20770
Tel.: 301-489-1776 Fax: 301-489-1660

Ms. Terry Walsh Roberts
Executive Director
The Governor's Office of Crime
Control & Prevention
300 East Joppa Road, Suite 1105
Towson, MD 21286-3016
Tel.: 410-321-3521 Fax: 410-321-3116

MASSACHUSETTS

Mr. Luis Garcia
Director of Planning and Research
Boston Police Department
154 Berkeley Street, Room 211
Boston, MA 02116
Tel.: 617-343-4531 Fax: 617-343-5011

Mr. Jonathan M. Petuchowski
Executive Director
Executive Office of Public Safety
100 Cambridge Street, Room 2100
Boston, MA 02202
Tel.: 617-727-6300 X301 Fax: 617-727-5356

MICHIGAN

Mr. Thomas Ginster
Interim Director
Office of Drug Control Policy
Michigan National Tower, Suite 1200
124 W. Allegan Street
Lansing, Ml 48909
Tel.: 517-373 4700 Fax: 517-373-2963

MINNESOTA

Mr. Steve Holmquist
Director
Stearns County, County Services
705 Court House Square, #445
St. Cloud, MN 56302-4773
Tel.: 612-656-6160 Fax: 612-656-6161

Ms. Ann Jaede
Program Director
Office of Strategic and
Long Range Planning
300 Centennial Office Building
658 Cedar Street
St. Paul, MN 55155
Tel.: 612-297-2436 Fax: 612-296-3698

Ms. Kathy Trihey, *Director*
Arrowhead Juvenile Detention Center
1918 Arlington Avenue North
Duluth, MN 55811
Tel.: 218-722-7776
Fax: 218-722-0018

MISSISSIPPI

Mr. Herbert Terry
Director of Justice Programs
Div. of Public Safety Planning
P. O. Box 23039
Jackson, MS 39225-3039
Tel.: 601-359-7896
Fax: 601-359-7832

MISSOURI

Mr. Gary B. Kempker, *Director*
Department of Public Safety
Truman State Office Building
P. O. Box 749
Jefferson City, MO 65102-0749
Tel.: 314-751-4905 Fax: 314-751-5399

MONTANA

Mr. Gene Kiser, *Director*
Montana Board of Crime Control
303 North Roberts
Scott Hart Building
Helena, MT 59620
Tel.: 406-444-3604 Fax: 406-444-4722

NEBRASKA

Mr. Allen L. Curtis
Executive Director
Commission on Law Enforcement an
Criminal Justice
301 Centennial Mall South
P. O. Box 94946
Lincoln, NE 68509-4946
Tel.: 402-471-2194 Fax: 402-471-2837

NEW HAMPSHIRE

Mr. Mark C. Thompson
Director of Administration
Department of Justice
Office of the Attorney General
25 Capital Street
Concord, NH 03301-6397
Tel.: 603-271-1234 Fax: 603-271-2110

NEW JERSEY

Mr. Thomas J. O'Reilly
Administrator
Department of Law and Public Safety
Office of the Attorney General
Richard Hughes Justice Complex
3rd Floor, CN 081
Trenton, NJ 08625
Tel.: 609-292-9660 Fax: 609-292-8268

NEVADA

Mr. James P. Weller, *Director*
Department of Motor Vehicles &
Public Safety
555 Wright Way
Carson City, NV 89711-0900
Tel.: 702-687-5375 Fax: 702-687-6798

NEW YORK

Mr. Jerome E. McElroy (RR)
Executive Director
NYC Criminal Justice Agency, Inc.
52 Duane Street, 3rd Floor
New York, NY 10007
Tel.: 212-577-0505 Fax: 212-577-0586

Mr. Paul Shechtman
Director of Criminal Justice
& Commissioner
NYS Div. of Criminal Justice Svcs.
Executive Park Tower
Stuyvesant Plaza
Albany, NY 12203
Tel.: 518-457-6086 Fax: 518-457-3089

NORTH CAROLINA

Mr. Richard H. Moore, *Secretary*
Department of Crime Control
& Public Safety
Room 234, Archdale Building
512 North Salisbury Street
Raleigh, NC 27611
Tel.: 919-733-2126 Fax: 919-733-0296

OHIO
Mr. Michael L. Lee, *Director*
Office of Criminal Justice Services
400 East Town Street, Suite 120
Columbus, OH 43215-4242
Tel.: 614-466-0280 Fax: 614-466-0308

OKLAHOMA
Ms. Gayle Caldwell
Grants Administrator
District Attorneys Council
2200 Classen Boulevard
Suite 1800
Oklahoma City, OK 73106-5811
Tel.: 405-521-2349 Fax: 405-524-0581

OREGON
Mr. LeRon R. Howland
Superintendent
Oregon State Police
400 Public Service Building
Salem, OR 97310
Tel.: 503-378-3720 X4100 Fax: 503-378-8282

PENNSYLVANIA
Mr. James Thomas
Executive Director
Commission on Crime and Delinquency
P.O. Box 1167
Federal Square Station
Harrisburg, PA 17108-1167
Tel.: 717-787-2040 Fax: 717-783-7713

Mr. Clay Yeager, *Director*
Center for Juvenile Justice
Training & Research
Horton Hall
Shippensburg University
Shippensburg, PA 17257
Tel.: 717-532-1704 Fax: 717-532-1236

PUERTO RICO

The Hon. Pedro R. Pierluisi
Attorney General of Puerto Rico
Office of the Attorney General
P. O. Box 192
San Juan, PR 00902-0192
Tel.: 809-721-7700 Fax: 809-724-4770

RHODE ISLAND

Mr. Joseph E. Smith
Executive Director
Rhode Island Governor's Justice
Commission
One Capitol Hill, 4th Floor
Providence, Rl 02908-5803
Tel.: 401-277-4493 Fax: 401-277-1294

SOUTH CAROLINA

Mr. William P. Collier, Jr.
Program Administrator
Criminal Justice Programs
SC Department of Public Safety
5400-4410 Broad River Road
Columbia, SC 29210-4088
Tel.: 803-896-8702 Fax: 803-896-8393

TEXAS

Ms. Karen J. Greene, *Executive Director*
Criminal Justice Division
Office of the Governor
P. O. Box 12428, Capitol Station
Austin, TX 78711
Tel.: 512-463-1952 Fax: 512-475-2440

UTAH

Ms. S. Camille Anthony, *Executive Director*
Utah Commission on Criminal and
Juvenile Justice
State Capitol, Room 101
Salt Lake City, UT 84114
Tel.: 801-538-1056 Fax: 801-538-1024

VERMONT

Mr. A. James Walton, Jr.
Commissioner of Public Safety
State Department of Public Safety
Waterbury State Complex
103 South Main Street
Waterbury, VT 05671-2101
Tel.: 802-244-8718 Fax: 802-244-1106

VIRGINIA

Mr. Bruce C. Morris, *Director*
Virginia Department of Criminal
Justice Services
805 E. Broad Street
Richmond, VA 23219
Tel.: 804-786-8718 Fax: 804-371-8981

VIRGIN ISLANDS

Mr. Ramon S. Devaila
Drug Policy Advisor to the Governor
Law Enforcement Planning Commission
8172 Sub Base, Suite 3
St. Thomas, VI 00802-5803
Tel.: 809-774-6400 Fax: 809-774-3317

WASHINGTON

Mr. Glenn A. Olson
Senior Executive Policy Coordinator
Statistics Analysis Center
Office of Financial Management
450 Insurance Building
Mail Stop AQ-44
Olympia, WA 98504
Tel.: 360-586-2501 Fax: 360-S86-4837

WISCONSIN

Mr. Steven D. Sell, *Executive Director*
Wisconsin Office of
Justice Assistance
222 State Street, Second Floor
Madison, WI 53702
Tel.: 608-266-7488 Fax: 608-266-6676

WEST VIRIGINIA

Mr. James M. Albert, *Director*
Criminal Justice and Highway
Safety Division
1204 Kanawha Boulevard East
Charleston, WV 25301
Tel.: 304-558-8814 Fax: 304-558-0391

WYOMING

Mr. Scott Farris
Intergovernmental Affairs
Coordinator
Governor's Office
State Capitol
Cheyenne, WY 82002
Tel.: 307-777-7437 Fax: 307-632-3909

23.0   U.S. GOVERNMENT AGENCIES

Among the efforts by various U.S. government agencies, the Secretary of Commerce has established an "Interagency Committee to Assess the Impact of Crimes Against Business," comprised of representatives of the Departments of Justice, Transportation, Housing and Urban Development, Treasury, and Commerce. Also included are the Federal Deposit Insurance Corporation, the Federal Reserve Board, the Securities and Exchange Commission and the Small Business Administration.

The objective of the Committee is to investigate, report, and make recommendations for a Federal Government effort to reduce the impact of crime against business. To accomplish this objective, it is assessing the economic impact of *these crimes* and evaluating the effectiveness of the existing Federal programs.

The first phase of the Committee's work involved examining
(1) What federal data programs exist in the various agencies.

(2) Where the data and program gaps exist if they do exist.
(3) How to adjust the efforts to plug these gaps and build a complete and effective federal approach to the problem of crime against business.

Although the Committee can identify and make recommendations for the main preventive and corrective efforts to be conducted by the Federal agencies, a continuing concern is required for the impact of crime on specific types of business activities.

To meet this need, the release of the second phase of the Committee's work in various publications shows the pertinent data and preventive techniques which affect the individual business sectors. The Committee's series of publications are geared to alleviate crime within these various sectors.

The work of this Committee is helping business and government to make a substantial contribution by increasing the public's awareness of the problem and assisting in a positive deterrent with protective actions.

BIBLIOGRAPHY

Addis, Karen K., *WHEN EMPLOYEES BEAT THE SYSTEM*, Security Management, V.35,#9, September 1991.

Almar Report, *HOW TO REDUCE BUSINESS LOSSES FROM EMPLOYEE THEFT AND CUSTOMER FRAUD*, Almar Press, Vestal, NY, First Edition, 1985.

Astor, Saul D. *PREVENTING RETAIL THEFT*, Small Business Administration Small Marketers Aids No. 119, Washington, DC, No Date.

Astor, Saul D., *PREVENTING EMPLOYEE PILFERAGE*, Small Business Association Management Aids No. 209, Washington, DC, No Date.

Barr, Peter B. and Phillip W. Balsmeier, *LOSING DOUGH IN BAKERIES*, Security Management, V32,#3, March 1988.

Bureau of Justice Statistics Special Report, *WHITE COLLAR CRIME*, U.S. Department of Justice, Washington, DC, 1987.

Clark, John P. and Richard C. Hollinger, *THEFT BY EMPLOYEES IN WORK ORGANIZATIONS*, National Institute of Justice, Washington, DC, September 1983.

Colombo, Allan B., *COVERT SURVEILLANCE: THE ISSUES UN-VEILED*, Security Distribution & Marketing, Vol 26, No.3, March 1996.

Cooney, Caroline M., *WHO'S WATCHING THE WORKPLACE*, Security Management, V35,#11, November 1991.

D'Addano, Francis, *SECURITY TURNS A PROFIT AT HARDEE'S*, Security Management, V37,#2, February 1993.

Elsberry, Richard B., *VIOLENCE, MURDER, THEFT, SABOTAGE, VANDALISM, RAPE*, Office Systems 96, May 1996.

Gaines, Leigh, *STEPS TO CUT EMPLOYEE THEFT*, Security, V25,#3, March 1988.

Gaines, Leigh, *TRAINING TOP SECURITY*, Security, V26,#2, February 1989.

Hampton, Steven, *SECURITY SYSTEMS SIMPLIFIED*, Paladin Press, Boulder, CO, 1992.

Hemphill, Charles F. Jr., *MODERN SECURITY METHODS*, Prentice-Hall, Inc., Englewood Cliffs, NJ, 1979.

Hughes, Mary M., Editor, *SUCCESSFUL RETAIL SECURITY*, Butterworth Publishers, Woburn, MA, 1978.

Inbau, Fred E., *INTEGRITY TESTS AND THE LAW*, Security Management, January 1994.

Insurance Information Institute, *$4 BILLION "SHRINKAGE" IN RETAIL STORE MERCHANDISE SWELLS POCKETS OF SHOPLIFTERS AND DISHONEST EMPLOYEES*, News Release, New York, No Date.

Jaspan, Norman, *BREAKING THE ADDICTION*, Security Management, V32,#4, April 1988.

Kline, John B., *MANAGEMENT AUDIT FOR SMALL MANUFACTURERS*, Small Business Management Series No. 29, Small Business Administration, Washington, DC, 1977.

Kolodny, Leonard, *OUTWITTING BAD CHECK PASSERS*, Small Business Administration Small Marketers Aids, No. 137, Washington, DC, No Date.

Landis, Brook I., *UNDERCOVER OPERATIVES AND THE CRUX OF CREDIBILITY*, Security Management, V33,#6, June 1989.

Lary, Banning K., *THIEVERY ON THE INSIDE*, Security Management, V32,#5, May 1988.

Law Enforcement Assistance Administration, *DETERMINATION OF UNDISCLOSED FINANCIAL INTEREST — AN OPERATIONAL GUIDE TO WHITE COLLAR CRIME ENFORCEMENT*, U.S. Department of Justice, Washington, DC, June 1979

Loffel, Egon W., *PROTECTING YOUR BUSINESS*, David McKay Company, Inc., New York, NY, 1977.

Masuda, Barry, *CARD FRAUD: DISCOVER THE POSSIBILITIES*, Security Management, V35,#12, December 1992.

Murphy, Joan H., *A TAILOR-MADE LOSS PREVENTION PROGRAM*, Security Management, V32,#8, August 1988.

National Institute of Standards and Technology, *COMPUTER SECURITY PUBLICATIONS, NIST* Publications List 91, Washington, DC, Revised February 1995.

Pankau, Edmund J., *BEATING BANK FRAUD*, Security Management, V32,#11, November 1988.

Ruder, Brian and J.D. Madden, *AN ANALYSIS OF COMPUTER SECURITY SAFEGUARDS FOR DETECTING AND PREVENTING INTENTIONAL COMPUTER MISUSE*, Computer Science & Technology, U.S. Department of Commerce, Washington, DC, NBS Special Publication 500-25, January 1978.

Shepard, Ira M., and Robert Duston, *THIEVES AT WORK: AN EMPLOYER'S GUIDE TO COMBATING WORKPLACE DISHONESTY*, The Bureau of National Affairs, Washington, DC, 1988.

Sherer, Michael, *WHEN IT'S NOT "ON THE HOUSE"*, Security Management, V34,#3, March 1990.

The Council of Better Business Bureaus, *HOW TO PROTECT YOUR BUSINESS*, The Benjamin Company,Inc., White Plains, NY, 1991.

U.S. Department of Commerce, *THE COST OF CRIMES AGAINST BUSINESS*, Bureau of Domestic Commerce, Washington, DC, Revised 1976.

U.S. Department of Commerce, *CRIMES AGAINST BUSINESS, A MANAGEMENT PRESPECTIVE*, Proceedings of Seminars Held in New York, NY, September 14, 1976

U.S. Department of Commerce, *CRIME IN SERVICE INDUSTRIES*, Domestic and International Business Administration, Washington, DC, September 1977.

U.S. General Accounting Office, *EMPLOYEE MISCONDUCT, JUSTICE SHOULD CLEARLY DOCUMENT INVESTIGATIVE ACTIONS*, Washington, DC, No. GAO/GGD-92-31, February 1992.

U.S. General Accounting Office, *BANK AND THRIFT CRIMINAL FRAUD, INFORMATION ON JUSTICE'S INVESTIGATIONS AND PROSECUTIONS*, Washington, DC, No. GAO/GGD-93-10FS, October, 1992.

U.S. Office of Consumer Affairs, *CONSUMER'S RESOURCE HANDBOOK*, The White House, Washington, DC, 1984.

VanDeMark, Robert L., *CONTROLLING INVENTORY IN SMALL WHOLESALE FIRMS*, Small Business Administration, Washington, DC, No. 122, 1973.

Verrill, Addison H., *REDUCING SHOPLIFTING LOSSES*, Small Business Administration Management Aids, Washington, DC, No.3.006, 1986.

Wels, Byron, *FIRE & THEFT SECURITY SYSTEMS*, Tab Books, Blue Ridge Summit, PA, 1976.

Zalud, Bill, *WINNING IT BACK IN COURT*, Security, V25,#8, August 1988.

Zalud, Bill, *WHAT'S HAPPENED TO SECURITY*, Security, V27,#1, September 1990.

INDEX

NOTES

NOTES

NOTES